Me and My Shadow

by Arthur Dorros

SCHOLASTIC
HARDCOVER

SCHOLASTIC INC.

New York

For
Claire
—A.D.

Many thanks to Dr. Donna L. Gresh,
Center for Radar Astronomy at Stanford University,
for her help in preparing this book.

Library of Congress Cataloging-in-Publication Data

Dorros, Arthur.
Me and my shadow.
Summary: Explains what shadows are, how and when they
exist, and how they reveal the size and shape of things
around us.
1. Shades and shadows — Juvenile literature.
[1. Shadows] I. Title.
QC381.6.D67 1990 535'.32 89-10100
ISBN 0-590-42772-5
12 11 10 9 8 7 6 5 4 3 2 1   0 1 2 3 4 5/9

Printed in the U.S.A.   36
First Scholastic printing, March 1990
Designed by Claire Counihan

Me and My Shadow

On sunny days, my shadow walks with me.
When I jump, my shadow jumps.
When I run, my shadow runs too.
Sometimes it's tall, sometimes it's small,
but it follows along with me.

Houses have shadows.
Cars and buses have shadows.
Trees have shadows.
Even my little brother and
the swing have a shadow!

See how many shadows you can find.
Trace around them.
Each shadow has a shape of its own.

What makes shadows?
Shadows are made when light is blocked from a surface.
Hold your hand out in bright sunlight,
or in front of a flashlight in a dark room.
There's the shadow of your hand.

Hold out a book, or a bear, or a piece of paper.
Whatever blocks the light makes a shadow.

ALLIGATOR
SHOES

If you hold the flashlight in different places you can see the shapes of shadows change. Shadows get bigger or smaller and change shape, depending on how the light is blocked.

When the sun is low, in the morning or afternoon,
a lot of light is blocked.
Then the shadow is tall.
When the sun is overhead, around the middle of the day,
not much light is blocked from the ground.
Then the shadow is shorter.

Shadows can also move.
Try catching them in a game of shadow tag.

Look at shadows.
Shadows help us tell what shape something is.
Try drawing an apple, a face, or tree bark,
with and without shadows.

There are shadows all around us.
A gigantic shadow is what gives us day and night.
The earth is like a big ball that spins in space.
As our part of the earth spins toward the sun,
we have day.
When our part of the earth is in the shadow,
we have night.

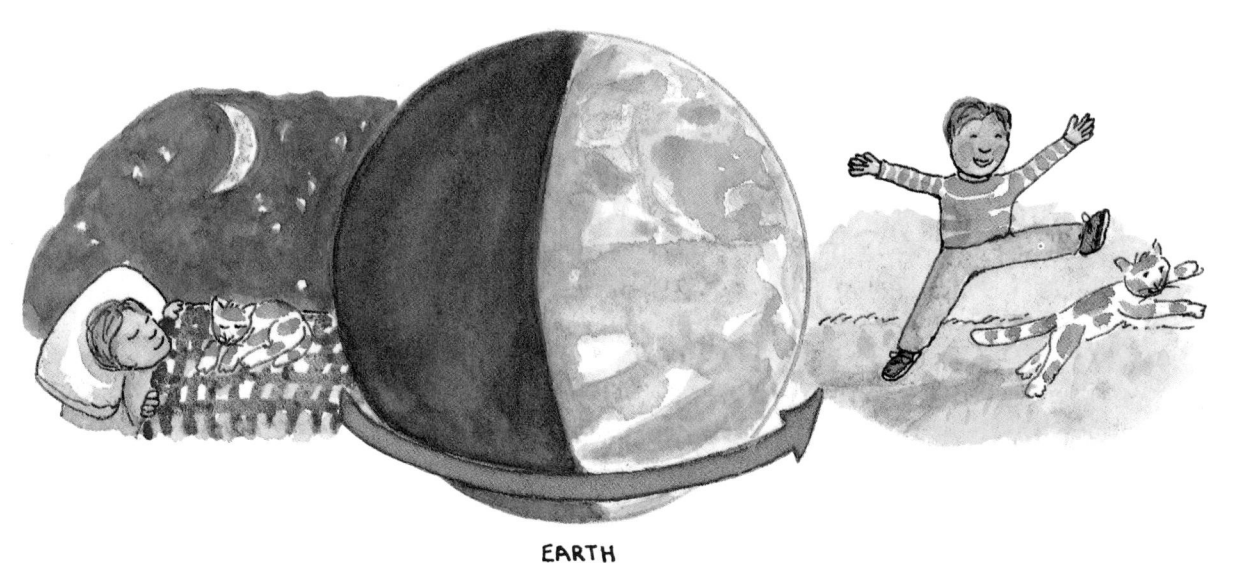

EARTH

SUN

You can see how this happens.
Shine a flashlight on a ball in a dark room.
On the side of the ball that is away from the light
there is a shadow.
On this side, it is nighttime.

The moon has a shadow too.
The moon circles the earth.
One half of the moon always faces the sun.
It is lit up.
The side away from the sun is always dark.
It is the shadow side of the moon.

The moon takes many days and nights
to circle the earth.
Each night, depending on where the moon is in its circle
around the earth, we see a different amount
of the moon's shadow and its lit-up side.

MOON

EARTH

SUN

On this night, the moon looks like just a sliver.
That is because we are seeing more of the moon's shadow
and less of the lit-up side than on other nights.
On nights that the moon looks round and full,
we are seeing more of the lit-up side and less shadow.

As the moon circles the earth, once in a while
it gets right between the sun and the earth.
Then the earth is in the moon's shadow—
we have an eclipse!

We can see how this happens in a dark room.
Cut out two round pieces of paper.
Shine a flashlight on them, like this:

But eclipses don't happen often.
Most nights I can see the moon and the shadows on its surface.
And most days, I see shadows in the sunlight.

In the morning when I wake up,
I see shadows on the ceiling.
The shadows are from parts of the window,
and anything that blocks the light.
Today I had a mountain lion in my room!

It's easy to tell stories with shadows.
You can make shadows on the wall by making shapes
with your hands in front of a strong light.
Walls come in handy for putting on shadow-puppet plays.

If you want to try something fancy,
make your own shadow-puppet theater.
You need a few pieces of thick paper,
a cardboard box, scissors, and tape.
Here's what to do:

Set up a puppet stage using a big sheet
of light-colored paper, or a thin cloth.
Cut the bottom of the box,
and tape the paper or cloth onto it.
Put a slide projector (or another strong light source)
behind the stage.
Turn off the other lights in the room,
and let your puppets tell the story!

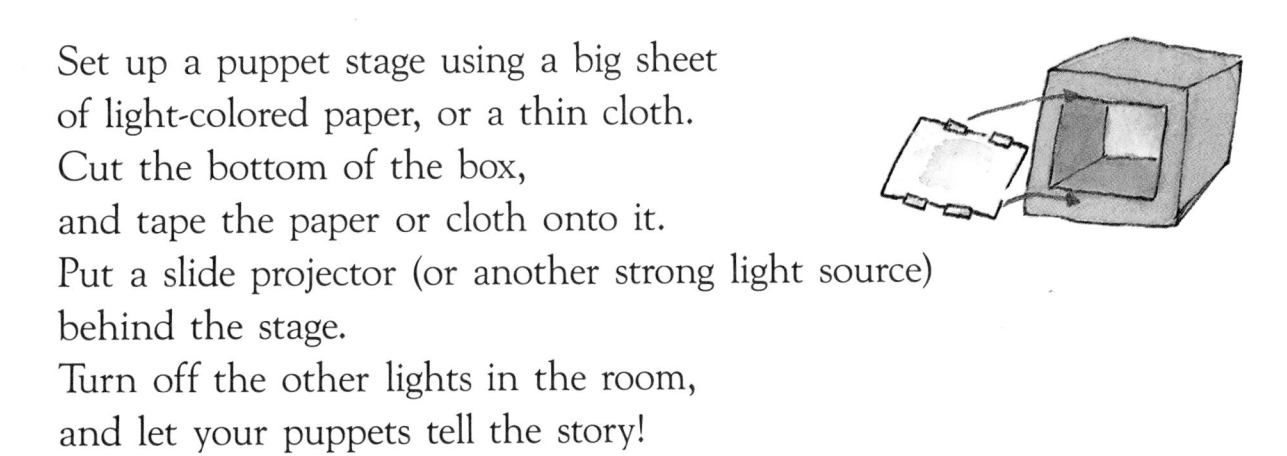

X rays are a way of using shadows too.
The rays go through us and make shadows
of our bones on film.

The film is developed, like film from a camera.
Shadows show on the developed film.
Where the X rays hit the film, the film turns dark.
Where the X rays are blocked by the bones,
there are white shadows.

X rays work because the rays pass through some parts
of things more easily than others.
Shadow pictures from X rays can be taken of almost anything.

Sonograms, pictures made by using sound,
also leave shadows.

Sound waves travel from a machine through water or air.
The sound waves bounce back when they hit something,
and show on a screen.
Behind whatever the waves hit there is a sound shadow.

Take a look—there are short shadows, tall shadows, round shadows, fuzzy shadows, shadows that move.

On a hot summer day,
I rest in the cool shadow of a tree.
I lie in the shade and watch
the shadows all around me!